Ezekiel 38-39

Turning Point

to the

70th Week

ERIKA GREY

Pedante Press

Short Book Series

005

DEDICATION

To my readers

CONTENTS

TWO PART SERIES

This short book is in two parts, the second work titled, "Messiah vs. False Messiah Israel's Covenant of Death follows this one.

www.erikagrey.com

For Bible Prophecy news and analysis and more books visit my website. For Bible Prophecy Updates on video subscribe to my YouTube channel Prophecy Talk with Erika Grey.

1 EZEKIEL 38-39 WAR

Ezekiel is among the major Biblical prophets. He lived during the sixth century and was also a Hebrew priest. God called him to be a prophet during the Babylonian exile. He served God at the same time as the prophet Jeremiah. The book of Ezekiel details an especially important end time prophecy known as the Ezekiel 38-39 war. Coincidentally Judaism also includes this conflict among their end time teachings

The Ezekiel 38-39 war predicts a massive coalition attack against Israel. It is spearheaded by the prince of Rosh of the land of Gog and Magog. Scholars identify the prince as Russia and the nations in the coalition as the Arab countries. Therefore, they refer to this war as the Russian/Arab invasion of Israel. Today Russia is in alliances with all the key nations mentioned. Other areas of the prophecy are also unfolding, that this report will discuss.

Ezekiel forecasts the nations descending upon Israel like a cloud. God miraculously defeats this massive collation. It takes seven years for the Israelites to burn all the weaponry and gear. When Ezekiel prophesied this war coalition forces of this distance were not possible. Instead warring empires aligned with neighboring tribes to fight others and expand their territory. At the time of this forecast, the major empires had been the Egyptian, Neo-Assyrian, and Babylonian.

Timeframe of the War

While the Ezekiel 38-39 war is a known Biblical prophecy, scholars do not agree on its timeline. Some believe it will occur before the Tribulation and others that this war marks the millennial kingdom. It is evident that this attack begins and kickstarts the Tribulation. It not only happens before it, but it provides the basis for the Antichrist's peace treaty and the rebuilding of the Third Jewish Temple. The start of the war also ends what Evangelicals refer to as the Church age, coincides with the sealing of the 144 thousand and Rapture of the church, and begins the final seven plus year dispensation. God's focus will again be on Israel.

Prior to the restoration of Israel as a nation, the Ezekiel 38 war was not even a possibility. In addition, during the era of the Soviet Union, many of the alliances described were not in place. After the fall of the iron curtain all of this changed.

The Coalition of Nations

We will look to see the details of the Ezekiel 38 forecast with first examining the coalition of nations in the war. Keep in mind that when the Bible mentions nations, it regards them from their earliest history or the time they first appeared in ancient Israel's past and names their founders. Ezekiel 38: 1-6 reads:

Now the word of the LORD came to me, saying, "Son of man, set your face against Gog, of the land of Magog, the prince of Rosh, Meshech, and Tubal, and prophesy against him, and say, 'Thus says the Lord GOD: Behold, I am against you, O Gog, the prince of Rosh, Meshech, and Tubal. I will turn you around, put hooks into your jaws, and lead you out, with all your army, horses, and horsemen, all splendidly clothed, a great company with bucklers and shields, all of them handling swords. Persia, Ethiopia, and Libya are with them, all of them with shield and helmet; Gomer and all its troops; the house of Togarmah from the far north and all its troops—many people are with you.

Sons and Grandsons of Noah

The nation's founders of the battle are the sons and grandsons of Noah. In 1 Chronicles Japeth is named as a son of Noah. His first born was Gomer, followed by Magog, Madai, Javan, Tubal, Mesheck, and Tiras. One of Gomer's sons is Togarmah. Each of these represent the territories they settled in. The passage reads, *"Adam, Seth,   Enosh, Cainan,   Mahalalel, Jared, Enoch,   Methuselah,   Lamech, Noah, Shem, Ham, and Japheth."*

The sons of Japheth were Gomer, Magog, Madai, Javan, Tubal, Meshech, and Tiras. The sons of Gomer *were* Ashkenaz, Diphath, and Togarmah. The sons of Javan *were* Elishah Tarshishah, Kittim, and Rodanim.

According to Chronicles, Magog, the second oldest son of Japhet is the prince of Mesheck and Tubal who were his younger brothers. Togarmah was the son of Gomer and nephew of Magog, Tubal and Meshceh.

The prince of Rosh

This is a northern nation mentioned with Tubal and Mesheck and is the Russians. Byzantine writers of the tenth century mentioned them dwelling north of Taurus or the Taurus mountain range in south central Turkey. The Russians are here meant, as one of the three Scythian tribes of whom Magog was the prince. The Greek's named them the Scythians. These were a group of ancient nomadic warriors who lived in what is now Southern Siberia. Their culture flourished around 900 BC to 200 BC and their influence extended all over Central Asia.

Gog

The land of the Rossi, Moschi and Tibareni or Tubal. These Scythians were in what is today Southern Russia, northern Turkey, and along the coast of the black sea.

The Moshchi or Moschoi: and the Georgian tribe of Meskhi is Georgia today. The tribes lived in the area of Georgia, which border's Russia's southern portion and lies just above Turkey's northeastern corner. These people were the ones referred to as the Scythians.

Land of Magog

Magog is a son of Japhet and became a great and powerful people inhabiting the extreme recesses of the North.

In Hippolytus of Rome's chronicle (234 AD), the "Illyrians" were identified as Meshech's offspring. Tubal, and Togarmah. According to Archibald Sayce, Meshech can be identified with Muska, a name appearing in Assyrian inscriptions, and generally believed to refer to the Mushki. The land of Magog is thought to be Russia.

Meshech

The descendants of Meshech are mentioned in connection with Tubal, Magog, and other northern nations. These also include the Moschi, a people on the borders of Colchis and Armenia. The Mescheck and Moschi, inhabited the Moschian mountains, between Iberia, Armenia, and Cochis, almost always joined with the neighboring Tibareni (Eze. 27:13, 32:26; 38:2, 3; 39:1.)

Tubal

The Tibareni, a nation of Asia Minor, dwelled by the Euxine (Black) sea, to the west of the Moschi. They are mentioned as early as the time of Herodotus and were believed to be of Scythian origin.

Persia

Persia is an empire located in southern Asia. It was created by Cyrus the Great in the 6th century BC. Alexander the Great destroyed it by the 4th century BC. At the time of the prophecy it encompassed the nations that would be today's Iran, Afghanistan, Pakistan, Turkmenistan and Turkey.

Ethiopia

Cush or Kush was, according to the Bible, the eldest son of Ham, a son of Noah (Gen 2;13, 10:608; Ezek. 38:5; I Chron 1:8-10.) Cush or Kush means Black. He was the brother of Canaan, Mizraim and Phut, and the father of the biblical Nimrod. The land occupied by the descendants of Cush are located around the southern parts of the Nile or Ethiopia. The Septuagint has two forms of the name and one means Ethiopia. The whole of East Africa was called Cush by the Greeks. This is the area of the Sudan today and possibly modern Ethiopia.

Libya

A nation or a people of Northern Africa: today's Libya. It is also called Put or Phut and is an African nation according to Josephus of Mauritania. The river Phut is mentioned by Pliny the Elder, a Roman author from AD 23 to 79.

Gomer

The Hebrew name Gomer refers to the Cimmerians, who lived in what is now southern Russia, "beyond the Caucasus'. They attacked Assyria in the late 7th century BC. Therefore, Gomer represents Southern Russia from Kazakhstan to Azerbaijan.

Togarmah

Togarmah is a northern country that derived from Gomer or the Cimmerians. They were abundant in horses and mules. Armenia is today known as the land of horses. The Armenians themselves regard Torgom, as the son of Gomer. They call themselves the house of Torgom. Therefore, Togarmah is Armenia and Turkey. These both border one another.

In the Ezekiel 38-39 coalition, while many of these nations settled in the area mentioned as far north, the remainder are in the Middle East and Africa. The passage is talking about this possible list of nations mentioned in Scripture:

Russia
Kazakhstan
Azerbaijan
Georgia
Armenia
Turkey
Iran
Afghanistan
Pakistan
Turkmenistan
Sudan
Libya or Northern Libya
Mauritania
Possibly Ethiopia
Possibly Ukraine
Possibly Belarus

There are Russia states not named in the Biblical account that fit into the prophecy. Such as the various "stan" nations. The Russian word for stan means settlement. The former stan countries have been mostly Turkic and speak languages from the Turkic family. Thus, the Biblical description "house of" Togarmah fits these nations.

2 THE NATIONS ALIGNING

Since the death and resurrection of Jesus, each historical event has led to the next with some bearing greater significance. Concerning Russia, during the reign of the Soviet Union, many pieces of the Ezekiel 38 prophecy were not in place. Since the fall of the Berlin Wall and dissolution of the Soviet Union many pieces of the Ezekiel 38 war fell into place. This includes the Jews who lived behind the iron curtain able to return to Israel.

Russia

Following the fall of the Soviet Union in 1991, The Commonwealth of Independent States formed. It cooperates in economic, political, and military affairs. In addition, it has certain powers relating to trade, finance, lawmaking, and security. From this organization is the

Commonwealth of Independent States Free Trade Area. Its members include:

Russia
Armenia
Belarus
Kazakhstan
Kyrgyzstan
Moldovia
Russia
Tajikstan
Ukraine
Uzbekistan

Collective Security Treaty Organization

In 1992, six post-Soviet states belonging to the Commonwealth of Independent States signed the Collective Treaty Organization. It has observer status at the UN General Assembly. Led by Russia, in 2002 they agreed to create it into an intergovernmental military alliance. Its purpose is to ensure the defense of any member that faces external aggression.

Its members include:

Russia
Armenia

Belarus
Kazakhstan
Kyrgyzstan
Tajikistan
Afghanistan
Serbia
Afghanistan-nonmember observer state
Serbia-nonmember observer state
Withdrawn states-Azerbaijan, Georgia and Uzbekistan

Eurasian Economic Union

In 2015 the Eurasian Economic Union formed. This is a market of 180 million people. Its organization mirrors the European Union. It encourages the free movement of goods and services. In addition, it operates through supranational institutions. Its members are:

Russia
Armenia
Belarus
Kazakhstan
Kyrgystan

The fall of the Soviet Union brought on good relations with nations of the Ezekiel 38 war, that had previously been strained.

PERSIA IRAN

The Soviet Union was the first State to recognize the Islamic Republic of Iran, in February 1979. During the Iran–Iraq War, however, it supplied Saddam Hussein with large amounts of conventional arms. Iran's Supreme Leader Ayatollah Khomeini deemed Islam principally incompatible with the communist ideals (such as atheism) of the Soviet Union.

After the war, especially with the fall of the USSR, Tehran–Moscow relations experienced a sudden increase in diplomatic and commercial relations, and Iran soon even began purchasing weapons from Russia. By the mid-1990s, Russia had already agreed to continue work on developing Iran's nuclear program, with plans to finish constructing the nuclear reactor plant at Bushehr, which had been delayed for nearly 20 years.

Since the fall of the Soviet Union, Russia and Iran have enjoyed close relations and are strategic allies. Russia is also a key trading partner for Iran and invited the nation to join its Collective Security Treaty Organization. This group which is the counter to NATO.

Russia and Iran also share a common interest in limiting the political influence of the United States in Central Asia. This common goal has led the Shanghai Cooperation Organization to extend to Iran observer status in 2005, and offer full membership in 2006. Iran's relations with the organization, which is dominated by Russia and China, represents the most extensive diplomatic ties Iran has shared since the 1979 revolution. Iran and Russia have co-founded the Gas Exporting Countries Forum along with Qatar.

Russia has also invited Iran to join the Eurasian Economic Union (EEU) and is currently working on a trade agreement.

Sudan

The Sudan is the second largest arms buyer in Africa. In 2017 half of Sudan's purchases were Russian. According to Giorgio Cafiero, the CEO of Gulf State Analytics, " TRT World, *"Russia's influence deepens as Sudan remains ignored by western powers,* "The Kremlin is positioning itself as indispensable to Sudan while it bids to increase its sway over Africa and Muslim countries." According to Debalini Ghoshal in her article in Gatestone Institute International

Policy Council, in August 2019, "Moscow has reportedly signed a "draft military agreement" with Sudan, "to facilitate entry of Russian and Sudanese warships to the ports of the two nations."

Russia also "is looking at establishing a logistics base in Eritrea" and has reached a "draft agreement with Egypt for Russian warplanes to use Egyptian military bases.

Ethiopia

Russia and Ethiopia have enjoyed over 120 years of diplomatic relations in economic, political, and global affairs. They share a mutual understanding in the international arena and a commitment towards each other's interests.

Libya

Relations between Russia and Libya are close and productive. Russia regarded the nation as one of its strongest allies in the Arab world. Russia expects to take part in the rebuilding of Libya when its civil war ends. It will also aid the sides in achieving a peaceful resolution.

Mauritania

Mauritanian is an Islamic republic with diplomatic relations with Russia. In addition, they share a trade agreement. July of 2014 marked the 50th year of their relations. In Russia's estimation their historical alliances unite them. The two sides have discussed views on settling the crisis in Syria and achieving progress in the Middle East settlement. These also include discussion on the Palestinian-Israeli track and resolving the conflict in the Sahara-Sahel region.

Russia Africa Union

The Russia Africa Summit in October of 2019 launched for the development of Russian African relations. They agreed to hold regular summits to coordinate policy on trade, security, investment, and research.

In May of 2020 Russia established the Russia-Africa Partnerships forum. The two sides aim to boost business links between the Russian and African companies. In addition, they will develop joint roadmaps for economic, academic, and cultural cooperation.

Turkey

Russian Turkish relations were hostile through the centuries. It was only since the 1920's these improved, but in 1952 Turkey joined NATO, the North Atlantic Treaty Alliance. It was established as a counter to the Soviet Union. In addition to providing collective security against it.

Distancing even further from Russia, in 1995 Turkey signed a Custom Union agreement with the European Union. Moreover in 1999 it was recognized as a candidate for full membership into the EU. In 2005 negotiations for EU membership began. Nevertheless, progress was slow and out of 35 Chapters necessary to complete the accession process, only one was opened and closed by 2016. The EU criticized Turkey for human rights violations. EU officials concluded that Turkish policies violated and did not meet the criteria for EU membership. In EU speak it is referred to as the Copenhagen criteria.

Meanwhile after the dissolution of the Soviet Union in 1991 their relations significantly improved. The two country's rank among each other's largest trading partners. Turkey is not a member of the Eurasian Union, it opted instead for a trade agreement with the EU. Although Turkey initially turned to the EU instead of Russia, it is now moving away from the European Union. This is now further strained since Turkey discovered a large gas field off its Black sea shore in 2020. This led to the Greece-Turkey conflict. In this Turkey is claiming vast areas of territory are its own and has NATO in a quagmire as both Greece and Turkey are NATO members. France is seeking sanctions on Turkey over the eastern Mediterranean gas exploration dispute. Turkey is rejecting Greece's maritime claims and stated that the EU had no basis for its stance. This provides yet another wedge and reason to further distance and get closer to Russia.

Turkey and Russia's Recent Relations

Turkish Prime Minister Recep Tayyip Erdogan met with Putin in May of 2009 and Putin stated, "stated, "Turkey and Russia have responsibilities in the region.

At the end of 2017 Turkey and Russia cooperated closely on ending Syria's civil war. In 2018 they backed each other against US sanctions. In 2017 Turkey announced it made a deal with Russia to purchase Russian 4-400 surface to air missile systems. The media viewed this as Turkey cementing its relations with Russia and moving away from NATO. Not to mention the purchase was in violation of NATO. In response the US canceled sending Turkey its stealth fighters, which Turkey is already courting Russia in purchasing.

We see a strengthening of Russian Turkish relations and also of Turkish Iranian relations in the last few years. Turkey is Iran's third largest export market. Turkey and Russia coming together more and more in preparation for the Ezekiel 38 battle.

Georgia

When Georgia regained independence in 1991, it sought to join NATO. Russia supported separatist regions within its state, which caused the nation to break ties. The Russo-Georgian War resulted. Both sides filed complaints in the international courts of each other committing war crimes.

In 2018 the Prime Minster of Georgia made a statement about the readiness of his nation to normalize bilateral relations with Moscow. In 2019 a Russian lawmaker's speech from the Georgian parliament speaker's chair prompted protests. Georgians are angry at Russia's occupation of the breakaway pro-Russian republics of South Ossetia and Abkhazia. Russia has suspended commercial relations with Georgia, which hurt it tremendously because the tourism industry of Russians visiting Georgia accounts for about 710 million dollars. Russia is a major export market and source of tourists.

Although Georgia and Russia's relations are conflictual, this will change as the timing for the war nears.

Ukraine and Belarus

Some scholars include Ukraine and Belarus. Currently they are engaged in a Russo-Ukrainian war following the Russian annexation of Crimea from Ukraine.

Belarus is having protests over its recent elections. President Lukashenko's win is considered fraudulent. He has good relations with Russia but the situation in Belarus is now questionable. So, these two nations both remain in question over their relations with Russia along with their participation in the war. If so, they will join the coalition.

One must also consider the following nations relations with each other along with Russia. This is not covered in this report but is an area worth looking into. Most significant is that the coalition is spearheaded by Russia and the nation is in alliance with each of the predicted members.

3 HOOKS IN JAWS

Many prophecy teachers when discussing Ezekiel 38-39 and current events highlight the conflicts of the Middle East as the road to fulfilling the prophecy. In addition to mentioning Russian aggression. On the contrary, based on the passage we are given the indication that Russia is in the opposite direction and is at peace with Israel and has good relations with the nation. The verse states, *"Thus says the Lord GOD: Behold, I am against you, O Gog, the prince of Rosh, Meshech, and Tubal. I will turn you around, put hooks into your jaws, and lead you out, with all your army, horses...."*

Significant here is the term, *"put hooks in thy jaws and lead you out,"* meaning that this war is not the normal course for Russia to take. It is brought about by the hand of God. God Himself turns the Russian leader around. The divine act is that God will send a spirit to influence the thoughts of the Russian president into forming this coalition. Ezekiel 38:10 predicts, "On that day it shall come to pass that thoughts will arise in your mind, and you will make an evil plan."

Fish in the Bible a Change of Direction

In the Ezekiel passage, *"hooks in the jaw"* is referring to the hooks to catch a fish. In the Bible fish symbolize a change of direction. We see this in the story of Jonah who God called to preach to the Ninevites, and he refused. God sent a whale to swallow him. Jonah was in the belly of a whale three days until he repented and changed direction.

The apostles were fisherman and became fishers of men. The early Christians used the symbol of a fish. Christianity is about a change of direction in one's life once they become born again. One leaves all behind to follow Jesus. It is no coincidence that fish in the Bible represent this turn.

Schools of fishes along with flocks of birds undergo sudden changes of their traveling direction. Fish's fins are designed to allow for the immediate switch of its path. In this passage, God is responsible for the big fish's reversal.

Hooks in Jaw of Pharaoh

We see this same meaning for Pharaoh recorded in Ezekiel. 29. It states:

"Behold, I am against you,
O Pharaoh king of Egypt,
O great monster who lies in the midst of his rivers,
Who has said, 'My River is my own;
I have made it for myself.'
⁴ But I will put hooks in your jaws,
And cause the fish of your rivers to stick to your scales;
I will bring you up out of the midst of your rivers,
And all the fish in your rivers will stick to your scales.

Further down in the passage we see the change of direction mentioned.

²⁸ Because your rage against Me and your tumult
Have come up to My ears,

Therefore I will put My hook in your nose
And My bridle in your lips,
And I will turn you back
By the way which you came.

As with Egypt, the Scripture emphasizes a change of direction by the Russian leader. What we would therefore expect to see as an end time sign is Russia establishing good relations with Israel. It is from these that God will turn Russia around.

Soviet Union's Hostile Relations with Israel

While initially the Soviet Union supported the creation of Israel, when the nation did not become an ally, the Soviet Union became hostile and a staunch Arab ally. This was after opposing the Israeli six-day war and afterwards arming Arabs. In addition, The Soviet Union would not allow Jews to emigrate to Israel. This stance did not need any turning around because the relations were not peaceful. In addition, the Jews living in the Soviet Union had not yet returned to Israel. This all changed after the fall of the Soviet Union and has been evolving.

The Transition

After so many Russian Jews immigrated to Israel in the 1990's, by 1999 former Israeli foreign minister Ariel Sharon began to embark on more friendly relations with Russia. In 1999 when Israel opposed the 1999 NATO bombing of Yugoslavia and supported IMF loans to Russia relations began to improve. It was with the election of pro-Israel Vladimir Putin that Russia embarked on a new diplomatic path with Israel.

Russia as Middle East Peacemaker

Russia's is now posturing itself as a peacemaker in the Middle East. This became evident when it joined the Middle East Quartet in 2002. It comprises of the UN, US, EU and Russia. Its purpose is to work together on steps to advance the Israel-Palestinian peace process. Since joining the Quartet, Russia has made further moves to establish itself as a peace broker in the region.

According to Al Jazeera's article, *Russia's Difficult Balancing Act Between Iran and Israel,* an opinion piece dated February 1, 2020 by Nikolay Kozhanov, an associate professor at the Gulf Studies Center of Qatar University as well as the senior research fellow at the Institute of World Economy and International Relations in Moscow stated that Russia has been pushing for improved Russia, Israel relations since the 1990s and added that under Netanyahu, Russia Israeli relations have flourished. He stated, "For years now, Russia has been striking a balancing act between Israel and Iran in the region. By 2015, the Kremlin managed to make Iran and Israel accept the fact that Moscow is not going to choose between them while being equally ready to develop cooperation with both."

According to Pritish Gupta of the Observer Research Foundation in his article, *"Russia and Israel: Towards a Pragmatic Partnership,"* "Russia and Israel have decided to improve their economic ties to expand trade between the two countries. Talks are underway for Israel to sign a free trade agreement with the Eurasian Economic Union." He stated:

"In 2015, Russia and Israel signed a military cooperation pact, to step up military and technological cooperation. Moscow also purchased a package of drones from Israel for USD 300 million. The presence of a large Russian diaspora in Israel has helped forge a special bond, with more than 17% of Israel's population being Russian speakers. President Putin made a statement last year that Russia believes Israel to be a 'Russian-Speaking Country.' Russia views them as 'sootechestvenniki' or compatriots."

During Vladimir Putin's speech at the 75th anniversary of Auschwitz Liberation. He essentially spoke against the seeds of antisemitism and stated, that "we must do everything to defend peace." Putin called for a meeting of the five UN Security Council members for that purpose. Russia's peaceful policy towards Israel is evident.

In 2020, Vladimir Putin backed a series of constitutional reforms that will allow Putin two more six-year terms. Thus, he can be in power until 2036 and might very well be the Prince of Rosh. Clearly Putin has secured peaceful relations with Israel. In addition, he has established Russia as a peace broker in the region.

Given Vladmir Putin's views towards Israel, God Himself will have to turn the Russian prince around into the direction of an attack against Israel. Examining Russia's current relations with Israel, it is now in the geopolitical position described in Ezekiel 38.

4 A TIME OF PEACE

The Bible is clear that the Ezekiel 38 war occurs when Israel is living in a time of peace. The passage predicts:

In the latter years you will come into the land of those brought back from the sword and gathered from many people on the mountains of Israel, which had long been desolate; they were brought out of the nations, and now **all of them dwell safely.** *⁹ You will ascend, coming like a storm, covering the land like a cloud, you and all your troops and many peoples with you."* *¹⁰ Thus says the Lord GOD: "On that day it shall come to pass that thoughts will arise in your mind, and you will make an evil plan:* **¹¹ You will say, 'I will go up against a land of unwalled villages; I will go to a peaceful people, who dwell safely,** *all of them dwelling without walls, and having neither bars nor gates'—*

Significant in this passage is that Israel dwells safely. Some scholars speculate that this era results from the Antichrist's treaty. The Antichrist is the forecasted man of sin who will sign a peace treaty with Israel, which begins the Tribulation period.

The 70th Week

The Tribulation or the 70th week of Daniel is the final period of God's judgements onto a wicked earth. It is seven-years of wars, plagues, famines, earthquakes, and disasters. It ends in the Battle of Armageddon, and the Second Coming of Jesus Christ. The Tribulation begins when the Antichrist makes a covenant with Israel (Dan. 9:27). His government will agree to act as the guarantor of the nation's peace. The Tribulation centers around Israel and God's focus is as in Israel's early history; on the Jews.

The Antichrist's Treaty is not this peace

For the scholars who have marked the Antichrist's treaty as bringing the peace in the Ezekiel 38 description, this is not possible because the Tribulation is seven years.

According to the passage the Israelites will burn the weapons for seven years. That would put the duration of the weapon destruction beyond the return of Christ. On the contrary, this battle ushers in the Antichrist's accord, more on that in a later chapter and in the second book of this series.

Prophecy Watcher's Errors on Conflicts

The attack occurs when Israel is living in a time of safety and this is further elaborated on. Israel is at peace with Magog and with the nations in the Middle East.

Many prophecy watchers have erroneously highlighted various conflicts and threats as unfolding the Ezekiel prophecy. On the contrary the Bible specifies a time of peace for Israel.

The Path to Peace Has Begun

In August of 2020 Israel and the United Arab Emirates agreed to an historic peace deal. This is only the third Arab country to agree to normalize ties with Israel. Egypt and Jordan being the first two. According to ABC News, *Israel and the United Emirates Make Historic Deal:*

"In that context it potentially starts to reshape relations in the Middle East, which have long been defined by enmity between the Arabs and the Israelis. "At the same time there were reports that Sudan had wanted to make peace with Israel as well. Right after the UAE agreement Bahrain followed with its own landmark deal with Israel. Bahrain in part made this deal because of the threat of Iran in the region.

According to Steven A. Cook, an expert who write for the Council on Foreign Relations, in his article, *What's Behind the New Israel-UAE Peace Deal?* He stated:

"The agreement between Israel and the United Arab Emirates promises to establish normal relations between the two countries. These include business relations, tourism, direct flights, scientific cooperation, and, in time, full diplomatic ties at the ambassadorial level." He added Oman and Morocco, in addition to Sudan and Bahrain might be the next candidates. President Trump stated in a press briefing that Kuwait might also be next. Trump has stated that seven, eight or nine nations might join. In addition, he suggested that this approach might lead to total peace.

Palestinian Issue

In Steven A Cook's article he highlighted both the Palestinian issue and that the Abraham Accord "enhanced security cooperation against regional threats, especially from Iran and its proxies." He pointed out that these existed before the agreement but are now formulized. He also mentioned, the treaty angering Palestinians and incorporating an agreement for Israel to stop annexing parts of the West Bank.

The Palestinian issue is over a century old, beginning at the turn of the 20th century when Jews started to return to their homeland. The idea of two states dates to the UN General Assembly before Israel became a nation in 1948.

The Six-Day War in 1967, ended with Israel occupying East Jerusalem, the West Bank and Gaza. Afterwards UN Security Council resolution 242, was adopted for Israel to withdraw from the lands to secure and recognize borders in exchange for peace. This righted the Palestinian cause. In addition, many nations adopted the two state policy as a solution. The Israel, Palestinian conflict has continued with many failed peace initiatives. This will need to come to resolution for Israel to experience the safety described in the Ezekiel passage. Donald Trump seems confident and suggested that the many nations now agreeing to normalized relations with Israel will lead to solving the Palestinian issue. The two-state solution is now viewed as unlikely and another proposal might gain acceptance.

Iran, Turkey and Pakistan

Iran has threatened to annihilate Israel. According to the July 15, 2020 Jerusalem Post article, *"Turkey is increasingly becoming a threat to Israel."* Turkey's Erdogan turned the museum of Hagia Sophia back into a mosque and stated that Ankara will liberate Al-Aqsa. Turkey also wants to unite the Islamic community against the State of Israel.

Both Turkey and Iran are part of Hamas: the Islamic political organization and militant group seeking to replace Israel with a Palestinian state. According to an interview with Al-Jazeera in August of 2020, After the UAE peace deal, "Pakistani Prime Minister Imran Khan stated that his country will not recognize Israel until there is a Palestinian State."

Israel's Mixed Relations with Iran, Turkey, Pakistan

Concerning Iran, Turkey and Pakistan, each country has had mixed relations with Israel. These countries have not always been a threat to Israel and the countries have held varying ties. Despite the calls for Israel's annihilation the Jews living in Iran are treated well and protected.

Turkey

Turkey was the first Muslim country to recognize the state of Israel. In the late 1990's Israel and Turkey signed a free trade agreement, and a bilateral investment treaty. Israel's defense force has helped to modernize Turkey's F-4 Phantom fleet of the Turkish air force. Agreements have included air, sea land and intelligence cooperation. In addition to manufacturing of aircraft, armaments and missiles, mutual military visits, and training. Not to mention and, dispatch of observers to oversee military exercises, staff exchanges and military know-how.

Pakistan

Pakistan and Israel extensively use their embassies and consulates-general in Ankara and Istanbul, Turkey to mediate and exchange information with each other. In 2017 Benjamin Netanyahu stated that Israel's partnership with India was not a threat to Pakistan by affirming, "We (Israel) are not enemies of Pakistan and Pakistan should not be our enemy either."

Peace Will Come

Evangelicals emphasize radical Islam's aim of annihilating Israel. While this is taught as the reason for the Ezekiel 38 war, on the contrary, we can expect to see these nations in time making peace with Israel. This of course as we get closer to the prophecy's fulfillment.

Benjamin Netanyahu stated, "There is an alignment of Israel and other countries in the Middle East that would have been unimaginable 10 years ago. Certainty in my lifetime, I never saw anything like it and I'm the same age as the State of Israel more or less, so its an extraordinary thing."

A video by VisualPolitic EN dated February 17, 2019 *The New Friendship Between Israel and the Arab Countries* stated, " These days, visits from the highest Israeli authorities to many Arab countries are turning into a common event; significant trade agreement are being signed and the security and defense ties are at unprecedented levels…Everything points to the likelihood that the Arab-Israeli conflict could soon become a thing of the past. Will there be a solution to that core Palestinian problem? "

Jews returning to their own land

The Ezekiel, 38-39 prophecy could not be fulfilled without Israel becoming a nation in 1948. In addition, Jews returning to their own land. This return began at the turn of the 20th century. The end of World War 11 brought in more. The fall of the Berlin wall allowed Jews who lived behind the iron curtain to return to Israel. They returned in historic numbers. More recent, the COVID-19 plague ushered a record 90k+ Jews returning to Israel during the period as the nations they lived in were falling apart economically due to COVID-19 and BLM riots.

5 TO TAKE A SPOIL

The Ezekiel 38 forecast provides the reason for the coalition attack. In addition, it describes the type of warfare. Essentially it launches the conflict to take the countries' goods it has acquired.   Its aim is to take it over for its products. The passage states:

12 to take plunder and to take booty, to stretch out your hand against the waste places that are again inhabited, and against a people gathered from the nations, who have acquired livestock and goods, who dwell in the midst of the land.

13 Sheba, Dedan, the merchants of Tarshish, and all their young lions will say to you, 'Have you come to take plunder? Have you gathered your army to take booty, to carry away silver and gold, to take away livestock and goods, to take great plunder?'

Its aim is not to destroy the nation

It should be noted that many expositors who relate Bible Prophecy to current events will point out that the Islamic nations stated purpose is to destroy the nation of Israel to support that we are in the current time frame, but on the contrary the Scripture is very clear that the perceived purpose of this invasion is not to destroy the nation on behalf of their faith but rather for its goods, but rather to take its booty.

Invasion-Annexation

Essentially a takeover. This will also act to acquire Israel's products. The overwhelming number of the army described as a cloud descending on the land will be a planned takeover like none other before it and on a grand scale to completely acquire the nation of Israel's industry's and goods. Possibly to annex Israel so that it is a part of Russia.

[14] "Therefore, son of man, prophesy and say to Gog, 'Thus says the Lord GOD: "On that day when My people Israel dwell safely, will you not know *it?* [15] Then you will come from your place out of the far north, you, and many

peoples with you, all of them riding on horses, a great company and a mighty army. [16] You will come up against My people Israel like a cloud, to cover the land.

Prior to the year 2000 Israel did not have substantial natural resources like the nations that are mentioned in the coalition. This all changed.

Discovery of Gas

In the year 2000, Israel discovered a small natural gas field located in offshore Ashkelon. Commercial production began in 2004. In 2009 a much bigger supply of gas was found in deep water west of Haifa, as well as a smaller field near the coastline. The discoveries of natural gas confirmed that the Levant basin of the Eastern Mediterranean contains significant quantities of natural gas. Test drilling and 3D Seismic surveys estimatec another large underwater geopolitical formation nearby the large gas field already discovered in 2009.

The discoveries revealed that Israel contains significant quantities of natural gas. Additional exploration off Israel's coastline continues.
In 2019 the New York Times reported that

Israel now had more gas than it could use or export. At one time Israel was an importer of natural gas, mostly from a pipeline in Egypt.

EastMed Pipeline

In January of 2020 Israel, Greece and Cyprus agreed to build an undersea pipeline to transport natural gas from its fields to Europe called the EastMed Pipeline. The pipeline will be in operation by 2025. Russia supplies 40% of the EU's gas, the 1300-mile EastMed line would supply 4%. The Israel pipeline will no doubt effect Russia's dominance in energy, which would be overtaken by the invasion.

According to Scott Carpenter's article that appeared in Forbes, *New Pipeline Deal gives Europe Access to Eastern Mediterranean Gas Reserves, Angering Turkey*: "Turkey is a key transit nation for supplies of Russian natural gas on their way to Europe, giving Turkey a source of leverage over Europe. New sources of European energy supply undermine that influence."

Turkish Gas Discovery

Turkey in the summer of 2020 discovered a

large gas field on the Black Sea, which would give it some leverage when getting pricing from Gazprom. In addition, the nation would only have to gain by the invasion as Turkey might view this as increasing its own advantage.

January 2020 Discovery Of Gold

In addition to Israel finding gas has been a recent discovery of gold. In the land of Ophir near the city of Eilat, private exploration company **Mirbatzei Zahav Ltd.** has made a significant gold discovery and is looking for investment partners to develop its property.

Archeologists speculate that King's Solomon's Mines might also be located at this mountainous region in southeast Israel. 1 Kings 9:28 states, *"And they went to Ophir, and acquired four hundred and twenty talents of gold from there and brought it to King Solomon."* According to their website:

Dating back to the biblical era, the land of Ophir – modern day surrounding mountains of the city of Eilat – has been the source of many armed conflicts between Egypt in the south, the Edomites in the east, and the Israelites in the north. What has made this remote desert land so important to everyone? The answer lies below the surface, in the rich metal deposits of the famous copper mines in Timna and the many surprising golden artifacts that were found in its vicinity. Minor gold explorations have been conducted by the State of Israel in the Roded Brook area, including: Wadi/stream sediment sampling, rock chip sampling on a grid, and two diamond drill holes to depths of 51 and 56 meters. Significantly anomalous gold was located in several areas, and gold values of up to ~2.8 g/t Au were determined in drill core.

History has shown that the Millstone Wadi has over 30 millstones and other archeological features related to the processing of gold bearing material early Islamic period.

Russia and Gold Reserves

According to US Global Investors article Top 10 Countries with Largest Gold Reserves dated, August 25, 2020, Russia is number five and "has been the largest buyer of gold for the past seven years and overtook China in 2018 to have the fifth largest reserves." According to an article that appeared in Bloomberg in March

2019, *Russia is stocking up on gold as Putin ditches US dollars*. It stated, "Vladimir Putin's quest to break Russia's reliance on the US dollar has set off a literal gold rush. Within the span of a decade, the country quadrupled its bullion reserves, and 2018 marked the most ambitious year yet." It will be in Russia's interest to also seek to acquire Israel's gold.

Israel's Science and Technology

In 2019 Israel ranked as the world's fifth most innovative country by the Bloomberg Innovation index. It is headquarters to major players in the high-tech industry. Israel is also home to many scientists.

Between the gas and gold, the prince of Rosh will have achieved a great plunder, let alone acquiring its technological sector.

Recently Syrian conservation sites and museums were looted during the Syrian civil war and their bounty was sold on the international black market. Many factory's in the rebels' zone of Aleppo were plundered and their assets transferred abroad. Agricultural production and electronic power plants were also taken to be sold. In the Ezekiel war it will also include Israel's scientific equipment.

The Soviets at the end of World War II plundered the Soviet Occupation Zone of Germany. They sent valuable industrial equipment, infrastructure, and whole factories to the Soviet Union. The great plunder would include so much more than overtaking gas and gold production. From Israel's scientific, industrial, and military weaponry are all among the items for the plunder. Israel is also home to artifacts and museums, and even more so the world's holy sites, which Russia would then control. Finally, the taking of the land of Israel itself.

The Size of the Army

To give you an idea of the size of this massive army, we will look at the populations of the country's involved. Note that the numbers are rounded up and meant to give an estimate. Russia's population is about 146 million, Turkey's 85 million, Iran 84 million, Pakistan 221 million, Sudan 44 million, Ethiopia 109 million, the remaining Stan nation's 20 million, Georgia 4 million, Armenia 3 million, not to mention the other nations involved. The population of the nations will number over 714 million. This constitutes a large massive army. If about 1% of these populations are soldiers, that constitutes a ground force of around 7.1 million soldiers. If the population of Israel is 8.7 million, this means the size of the army is not far off that of the population. No doubt numerous enough to take a spoil and more.

A Big Question

A question is when Russia embarks on this invasion, why it will not expect its attack to launch World War. Most likely because it will have the weight of so many nations. Russia will estimate that a weakened US could not possibly wage war with all the country's involved. Moreover, the dollar collapse might have occurred leaving the US with too many of its own internal problems. Russia will not expect the European Union to go into a world war over Israel but if it did it will feel prepared.

 If God did not intervene and defeat the coalition, the EU might have taken military action. But this does not occur because God Himself defeats this army. Russia would not expect China, India, or the other BRIC nations to retaliate for such an invasion. With the European Union it would be drawing a line in the sand by such an event. The EU will act after the defeat, and this is written about in part two or the follow up to this book.

Finally, this invasion will be conducted as a ground war, with many troops coming in from the dirt from the nations that border Israel. This strike will not involve nuclear warheads, missiles, or planes. The Nations coming from Africa will have to cross the Red Sea or fly to the other nations to join the ground forces. What is also striking is this is Russia's method of operation in Ukraine, by sending in ground troops. It is also how it entered Georgia. This is how Russia and its coalition will invade Israel but on a grander, more calculated scale.

6 SIGNIFICANCE OF SEVEN YEARS

As was stated earlier, theologians and Bible Scholars to not agree on the timing of the Ezekiel 38 war. Some say that it will occur during the millennial rein of Christ. Others that it will happen during the Tribulation. The view that this work proves is that is that it occurs prior to the start of the Tribulation.

During the rise of God and Magog in the millennium, they surround the beloved city and fire comes down and devours them as referenced in Revelation 20:8. This does not at all align with the details given in Ezekiel 38. Moreover, it is negated by the seven-year duration of events listed.

Burning of Weapons for Seven Years

While we have been examining this passage in

sequence, in this chapter we are going to jump ahead to the specified seven-year time frame. It reads:

⁹ "Then those who dwell in the cities of Israel will go out and set on fire and burn the weapons, both the shields and bucklers, the bows and arrows, the javelins and spears; and <u>they will make fires with them for seven years.</u> ¹⁰ They will not take wood from the field nor cut down any from the forests, because they will make fires with the weapons; and they will plunder those who plundered them, and pillage those who pillaged them," says the Lord GOD.

The burning of the weapons takes place for seven years. In today's warfare, weapons are made of metal. This burning is therefore not literal, but figurative and represents that the materials will be able to be recycled and provide value to Israel. Israel will not have to use its own resources for the financial benefits. It also gives the idea that the number of the soldiers is so numerous that it will take seven years to rid of all the weapons. Remember this was written in ancient text when the population was not as great as it is today. Neither the possibility for an army of about seven million. As the passage predicts, Israel will then plunder those who sought to pillage them.

This seven year of pillaging is also related to the seven-year tribulation that begins with the Peace treaty. In the Scripture we have other instances of numbers not exactly linking but that will shed light on the significance of the number. For instance, we have Revelation 13:16 of the name of the beast as number 666. We also learn that Solomon took in 666 shekels of gold, the 666 shekels of Gold that Solomon took in gives us clues to the meaning of the number 666 of Revelation that the number pertains to idolatry.

We see a similar instance of the number 30 of the chargers, the offering of 100 and 30 pieces of the mentioned in Zechariah 11:12-13:

Then I said to them, "if I is agreeable to you, give me my wages; and if not, refrain. So, they weighed out for my wages 30 pieces of silver. And the Lord said to me, throw it to the potter—that pricey price they set on me. So, I took the thirty pieces of silver and threw them into the house of the Lord for the potter.

The 30 pieces are referenced as "wages" reference the 3O pieces of silver that Judas was paid for betraying Jesus. We also see in Scripture the 10 days of Tribulation that Jesus mentions to the church in Smyrna in

Revelation 2:10, that "they shall have tribulation 10 days." We see the 10 days appear in the book of Daniel which compliments the Revelation. Daniel asks to be given ten days and the ten days of Daniel offers insight into the Ten days of Revelation, which I have written about.

So it is that the seven in this verse is used in the same context. In seven days, the earth was made, in seven years, God sends his judgments onto the earth and life on earth ends. Seven years conclude the final years for the nation of Israel. These reinforce not only God's seven-year time frame for Israel, but that He is with them in these years. It is also a hint that these years also align with the Tribulation.

These seven years do not line exactly with the start of the Tribulation but occur just before them. They provide the starting point; the transition to them. God is letting us know the time this happens in and that the seven years that follow God is the God of Israel, which then takes us to the end of the Tribulation.

The Ezekiel war cannot happen during the Tribulation because its duration is seven years until the battle of Armageddon.

Therefore, the Ezekiel 38 war would have to occur sometime before the start of the Tribulation. From the time of the battle until the Antichrist's peace treaty, which begins the Tribulation will have to take several months. This would give the seven-year period for the burning of the weapons.

At some point the seven-year burning of weapons will overlap the Antichrist's reign of terror, which starts at the abomination of desolation, the act Jesus warned about that begins the Great Tribulation.

The Literal Cleaning of the Land

The Bible provides exact details of the cleaning up of the land and this is literal, the seven months of sanitizing.

11 "It will come to pass in that day that I will give Gog a burial place there in Israel, the valley of those who pass by east of the sea; and it will obstruct travelers, because there they will bury Gog and all his multitude. Therefore they will call it the Valley of Hamon Gog. [e] 12 For seven months the house of Israel will be burying them, in order to cleanse the land. 13 Indeed all the people of the land will be burying, and they will gain renown for it on the day that I am glorified," says the

Lord GOD. [14] "They will set apart men regularly employed, with the help of a search party,[a] to pass through the land and bury those bodies remaining on the ground, in order to cleanse it. At the end of seven months they will make a search. [15] The search party will pass through the land; and when anyone sees a man's bone, he shall set up a marker by it, till the buriers have buried it in the Valley of Hamon Gog. [16] The name of the city will also be Hamonah. Thus they shall cleanse the land."'

We see the seven months of cleansing, like the seven years of the burning of the weapons. God is letting Israel know in no uncertain terms, that He is with them during these earth's final years.

7 TIMING OF RAPTURE & SEALING OF 144 THOUSAND

We have established that the Ezekiel 38 war occurs before the start of the Tribulation. It is apparent after careful examination of the passage that the battle ends what theologians regard as the church age. It also ushers in the Antichrist's peace treaty and provides the timing of the Rapture and the sealing of the 144 thousand Jews.

Church Age or Age of Grace

Theologians teach that the Church Age, sometimes referred to as the Age of Grace will end. But this is an incorrect theological term because God's grace does not end, neither does the basis for salvation of faith in Jesus Christ. What changes is that during the Tribulation the Antichrist will institute the mark of the beast. You will have a choice to take it and live or not accept it and die. If you take the mark, you will commit the blasphemy of the Holy Spirit that Jesus warned about in the Gospels. If the Holy Spirit is blasphemed, your sins are not forgiven. If you are saved and commit the act, the Holy Spirit must retreat. This is the only way your name can be blotted out of the Book of Life. Revelation 3:5, 17:8. For more on why taking the mark equates with blasphemy of the Holy Spirit see my book, *Decoding 666 The Number of the Beast.*

This means that after the start of the Tribulation, all believers who die naturally before the mark of the beast comes to fruition, will not have to make that choice, and suffer the torture and death for not taking it.

Blasphemy of Holy Spirit Applies to All

Therefore, salvation by faith does not end, only in the present age the means to blaspheme the Holy Spirit is not present. We can also lose our salvation by committing this unpardonable sin. The church age also does not end either. The book of Revelation depicts Jesus among the seven candlesticks and holding the seven stars in His hand. These represent the churches. One is Smyrna, which no doubt are the

Tribulation Saints. Smyrna at the time of the apostles had a considerable Jewish population. Most likely the church was nearly all Jewish believers and fits the last days Jewish church.

What will end is the period described in Roman's 11 and specifically mentioned in Romans 11:25 as "the fullness of the Gentiles." This is the current period - the grafting in of the Gentiles- that will come to its fruition at the start of the Ezekiel 38 war.

Sealing of the 144 Thousand

Revelation 7 provides a sequence of events that occur in chronological order. It begins with a stilling of the wind and the sealing of the 144 thousand Jewish witnesses. These are Jewish evangelists who will preach the gospel during the Tribulation. It reads:

7 After these things I saw four angels standing at the four corners of the earth, holding the four winds of the earth, that the wind should not blow on the earth, on the sea, or on any tree. ² Then I saw another angel ascending from the east, having the seal of the living God. And he cried with a loud voice to the four angels to whom it was granted to harm the earth and the sea, ³ saying, "Do not harm the earth, the sea, or the trees till we have sealed the servants of our God on their foreheads." ⁴ And I heard the number of those who were sealed. One hundred and forty-four thousand of all the tribes of the children of Israel were sealed:

The following four verses (4-8) list all the tribes that are sealed and gives the number.

The Rapture

When the final 144th witness is sealed, the Rapture occurs. This is God's removal of the mostly Gentile church as there are Jews who have accepted Christ. Revelation 7: 9 -10 confirms:

⁹ After these things I looked, and behold, a great multitude which no one could number, of all nations, tribes, peoples, and tongues, standing before the throne and before the Lamb, clothed with white robes, with palm branches in their hands, ¹⁰ and crying out with a loud voice, saying, "Salvation belongs to our God who sits on the throne, and to the Lamb!"

The Stilling of the Winds

The winds are held back in a stilling. John Dodgson of Phys.org reported in an article in 2017 titled, *The Stilling: global wind speeds slowing since 1960,* that winds are slowing. He called the phenomena a stilling. A brief stilling takes place while the 144 thousand are sealed. Simultaneously at the end of this event, the angels instantly release the winds and at this moment the troops are descending upon Israel as a cloud. Therefore, the sealing of the 144 thousand takes place at the very final hours of the Gentile Church age while the coalition troops are in route to Israel.

Once the final witness has been sealed, the four angels release the winds. Simultaneously the great earthquake takes place and signifies the end of the Gentile Church age. At the timing of the earthquake along with the other predicted cataclysmic natural events the believers are raptured out of the earth. They are listed in the passage: flooding rain, great hail, fire and brimstone.

21 I will call for a sword against Gog throughout all My mountains," says the Lord GOD. "Every man's sword will be against his brother. 22 And I will bring him to judgment with pestilence and bloodshed; I will rain down on him, on his troops, and on the many peoples who are with him, flooding rain, great hailstones, fire, and brimstone.

Several times in the Scriptures we see that when God works in mighty ways, events in nature occur. Around the throne room are thunders and lightening. Other examples in the Bible are the parting of the Red Sea, the earth swallowing the men of Korah, and the destruction of the earth by the flood. We can also add the Rapture of the Gentile church to this list. It will appear as if certain people just vaporized simultaneously with the earthquake, flooding rain, great hailstones, fire, and brimstone.

Brimstone is sulfur. Scientists theorize that Sodom and Gomorrah's destruction resulted from a massive meteor explosion above the earth. A similar one occurred in Russia over 100 years ago.

In addition to the fire and brimstone God will send fire on the coastlands, which indicates extreme heat causing fires. Ezekiel 39:6 predicts, *"And I will send fire on Magog and on those who live in security in the coastlands."* All these catastrophic events will take place simultaneous with the Rapture.

8 END OF GENTILE CHURCH AGE

Once God shows Himself to the nations and this event ends marks the end of the Gentile Church. It also ushers in the Tribulation and the 70th week of Daniel.

In the Bible, are time periods that theologians refer to as dispensations. When Jesus died on the cross the law officially ended when the veil of the temple was torn in two. The book of Matthew 27:51 records at the moment of Jesus's death," *Then, behold, the veil of the temple was torn in two from top to bottom; and the earth quaked, and the rocks were split.*"

 The sun also darkened on that day, which is recorded in three of the Gospels.

Significance of Earthquake

At the death of Jesus and the end of the law,

notice the events that occurred in nature particularly the earthquake. In the throne room of God, we see that from His throne emits thunders and lightening's and earthquakes. We see that that when God acts forces of nature accompany His actions. In addition, these events are significant.

It will be in the latter days that I will bring you against My land, so that the nations may know Me, when I am hallowed in you, O Gog, before their eyes." [17] Thus says the Lord GOD: "Are you he of whom I have spoken in former days by My servants the prophets of Israel, who prophesied for years in those days that I would bring you against them?

[18] *"And it will come to pass at the same time, when Gog comes against the land of Israel," says the Lord GOD, "that My fury will show in My face. [19] For in My jealousy and in the fire of My wrath I have spoken: 'Surely in that day there shall be a great earthquake in the land of Israel, [20] so that the fish of the sea, the birds of the heavens, the beasts of the field, all creeping things that creep on the earth, and all men who are on the face of the earth shall shake at My presence. The mountains shall be thrown down, the steep places shall fall, and every wall shall fall to the ground.'*

This cataclysmic earthquake is in line with the

one at Jesus's death that ended the law but this quake ends the era of the Gentiles and ushers in the 70th week of the Jews. This confirms the switch in dispensations or time periods. Paul confirms in Romans 11:25, *"For I do not desire, brethren, that you should be ignorant of this mystery, lest you should be wise in your own opinion, that blindness in part has happened to Israel until the fullness of the Gentiles has come in."* The earthquake occurs marking the completion of the number of Gentiles saved. In addition, the turning point from the grafted Gentiles to the Jews.

God miraculously defeats the massive Ezekiel 38 coalition. He in part accomplishes this through issuing the catastrophic weather that accompanies the earthquake. This will be so great it will destroy the Al-Aqsa mosque. Along with the strength of this earthquake and its predicted aftermath, the Rapture occurs simultaneously taking out those of the Gentile Church age that are alive to be caught up in the clouds.

This verse aligns with Revelation 6

As evidence that this battle begins the Tribulation, we see Ezekiel 38:21 compares with details given in Revelation 6:3. : Ezekiel

38:21 states, "...*Every man's sword will be against his brother.*" This lines with the four horsemen prediction in Revelation 6:3. It reads: *"When he opened the second seal, I heard the second living creature saying. Come and see, Another horse fiery red went out And it was granted to the one who sat on it to take pace from the earth, and that people should kill one another and there was given to him a great sword."* This killing of one another indicates that the Tribulation period has now started.

Another key passage that pinpoints the start of the final seven years is the statement, *"Thus I will magnify Myself and sanctify Myself, and I will be known in the eyes of many nations. Then they shall know that I am the LORD."'*

Another words, make no mistake, the God of Israel is back fighting on behalf of Israel, as in the days of the children of Israel's early history. Through this event He reappears. The transition, turning point or prelude of the 70th week has begun.

More Details on the Coalitions Defeat

The passage gives more details to the coalition's defeat. We see again that God directly deals with Israel's enemies. It states:

39 "And you, son of man, prophesy against Gog, and say, 'Thus says the Lord GOD: "Behold, I am against you, O Gog, the prince of Rosh,[d] Meshech, and Tubal; 2 and I will turn you around and lead you on, bringing you up from the far north, and bring you against the mountains of Israel. 3 Then I will knock the bow out of your left hand and cause the arrows to fall out of your right hand. 4 You shall fall upon the mountains of Israel, you and all your troops and the peoples who are with you; I will give you to birds of prey of every sort and to the beasts of the field to be devoured. 5 You shall fall on the open field; for I have spoken," says the Lord GOD.

The God of Israel is Back

The final passage further predicts and affirms that this event begins the final dispensation and God returning to Israel. God calls Himself, *"The Holy One in Israel* and God makes Himself known to the Israelites via the same miraculous acts as in their early history and the nation turns to Him. The age of the Gentile Church has ended. This is affirmed several times as we read on:

"Then they shall know that I am the LORD. 7 So I will

make My holy name known in the midst of My people Israel, and I will not let them profane My holy name anymore. Then the nations shall know that I am the LORD, the Holy One in Israel. ⁸ Surely it is coming, and it shall be done," says the Lord GOD. "This is the day of which I have spoken."

The Full Impact of This Miracle

To get the full impact of God's miracle we must consider that the army that invaded is nearly the size of Israel's population. During Israel's early history the numbers for any army would not be this great. More evidence the Ezekiel 38-39 fits in with our times.

In the following verses God provides more on this great defeat of the coalition:

¹⁷ "And as for you, son of man, thus says the Lord GOD, 'Speak to every sort of bird and to every beast of the field:
"Assemble yourselves and come;
Gather together from all sides to My sacrificial meal
Which I am sacrificing for you,
A great sacrificial meal on the mountains of Israel,
That you may eat flesh and drink blood.
¹⁸ You shall eat the flesh of the mighty,
Drink the blood of the princes of the earth,

Of rams and lambs,
Of goats and bulls,
All of them fatlings of Bashan.
¹⁹ You shall eat fat till you are full,
And drink blood till you are drunk,
At My sacrificial meal
Which I am sacrificing for you.
²⁰ You shall be filled at My table
With horses and riders,
With mighty men
And with all the men of war," says the Lord GOD.

God's Word in Israel From this day forward.

In the following passages God clarifies the beginning of the new dispensation, which is the earth's final seven years and it clearly is a time for Israel which matches the 70ᵗʰ week of Jeremiah the prophet. The message cannot be any clearer than in this final passage.

²¹ "I will set My glory among the nations; all the nations shall see My judgment which I have executed, and My hand which I have laid on them. ²² So the house of Israel shall know that I am the LORD their God from that day forward. ²³ The Gentiles shall know that the house of Israel went into captivity for their iniquity; because they were unfaithful to Me, therefore I hid My face from them. I gave them into the hand of their enemies, and they all fell by the sword. 24 According to their uncleanness and according to their transgressions I have dealt with them and hidden My face from them."'

25 "Therefore thus says the Lord GOD: 'Now I will bring back the captives of Jacob, and have mercy on the whole house of Israel; and I will be jealous for My holy name—26 after they have borne their shame, and all their unfaithfulness in which they were unfaithful to Me, when they dwelt safely in their own land and no one made them afraid. 27 When I have brought them back from the peoples and gathered them out of their enemies' lands, and I am hallowed in them in the sight of many nations, 28 then they shall know that I am the LORD their God, who sent them into captivity among the nations, but also brought them back to their land, and left none of them captive any longer.

And I will not hide My face from them anymore; for I shall have poured out My Spirit on the house of Israel,' says the Lord GOD."

In the pouring of the Spirit, the veil or blindness that the apostle Paul talks about has been lifted. The Spirit will help them in the days and horrific trials to come. Meanwhile the 144 thousand begin their evangelism and witness.

9 THE TRIBULATION BEGINS

Along with God's victory and defense of Israel the Tribulation officially has begun. His great power revealed in the victory of the Ezekiel 38 war will help the nation with what is coming. God reveals himself at the beginning of the Tribulation in a most miraculous way to both put His stamp on the days ahead as well as to provide a sign to the lost.

The Russian attack will also have fulfilled Jesus's words of nation rising against nation and kingdom against kingdom. This in addition to other conflicts of the birth pangs.

The great earthquake will destroy the Al-Aqsa Mosque allowing for the building of the Third Temple.

The Rapture of the church will be attributed to

the cataclysmic natural disasters that occurred during the Ezekiel 38 war. Scientists will have theories on how the people disappeared or in their estimation were vaporized. Theoretically strong enough lightning bolts can vaporize people. Maybe they will attribute it to a meteor. They will provide a scientific theory to explain the mass disappearance.

In Ezekiel 39:6 it states, *"And I will send fire on Magog and on those who live in security in the coastlands. Then they shall know that I am the Lord."* These will be produced by the sun and will be unlike any that has happened on the earth. Scientists might relate this event to the vaporization of those who exited in the Rapture. Or somehow to the great earthquake. The Rapture will have occurred during these events.

The path is now clear for the Antichrist to come onto the scene with the seven-year peace treaty, which to theologians officially begins the seven-year period of the Tribulation. The Antichrist will be sitting in his political seat and will blame the Rapture on Climate change, which he will champion to battle.

The Ezekiel 38-39 prophecy provides the

turning point from the church age to the 70'th week i.e. the seven years of the Tribulation. At the event God's focus directs back to Israel. In addition, we see that due to the events of the Ezekiel 38-39 war, other major predictions will result. Finally, the Ezekiel 38-39 prophecy provides the transition period from the Rapture, sealing of the 144 thousand to what is the key marker for the start of the Tribulation.

God sets the stage.

God Himself provides a miracle so great that there is no excuse for those who reject Him. During the Tribulation even after God's judgements begin Revelation 9:20 affirms, *"But the rest of mankind, who were not killed by these plagues, did not repent of the works of their hands, that they should not worship demons, and the idols of god and of silver and of brass and of stone and of wood, which can neither see nor hear nor walk."*

Even more so God sets the stage for the nation of Israel. The Antichrist is then given his opportunity to come on the geopolitical scene with his treaty and draw the Jews to himself.

For the continuation see part two of this short book titled, "Messiah vs. False Messiah, Israel's

Covenant of Death." In it are the details about the Messiah the Jew's have been looking for, what their rabbis teach about the Ezekiel 38 war, and how their teachings overlap with the Antichrist's actions. Finally, a comprehensive look at the Antichrist's Peace Treaty and what it will entail after the Ezekiel 38 war, along with the rebuilding of the Third Jewish Temple and more.

ABOUT THE AUTHOR

Erika Grey, author, Bible scholar, commentator, journalist has been a born-again Christian for over 40 years She has written numerous books on Bible Prophecy and made contributions in helping to decode the more difficult forecasts. She has spoken on numerous radio stations including Coast to Coast and interviewed high level policy makers.

This book is one of a series of short books by Erika Grey intended to be quick reads with important information. Be sure to check out Erika's other titles at www.erikagrey.com.